ENVIRONMENTAL SYST

CW01573092

Tropical Savannas

D. C. Money

Evans

Evans Brothers Limited

Published by Evans Brothers Limited
Montague House, Russell Square, London WCIB 5BX

Evans Brothers (Nigeria Publishers) Limited
PMB 5164, Jericho Road, Ibadan

First published 1980

Acknowledgements
Aerofilms, p. 42
J. Allan Cash, p. 26
Professor M. M. Cole, pp 13 (bottom), 35
All other photographs were taken by the author

Line illustrations on pp. 8, 12, 21 and 32 by the author
Other line illustrations by Reproduction Drawings

ISBN 0 237 29265 3   PRA 6921

Filmset and printed by BAS Printers Limited,
Over Wallop, Hampshire

Contents

Cover photograph The Olduvai Gorge in northern Tanzania has been cut through successions of lake deposits of clays, silts and sands, layers of volcanic ash, and red iron-enriched sandstones which, over a period of two million years, have accumulated above sheets of lava. The remains of prehistoric family life have been found in the lower levels.

The gorge and the surface into which it has been cut illustrate the fact that climate alone does not produce specific forms of savanna vegetation. Beyond the gorge, almost treeless grasslands, heavily grazed and trampled by wildebeeste and zebra, cover the pervious layers of sands and ash. But the slopes within the gorge bear a variety of trees, shrubs and grasses. There the vegetation responds to seepage and drainage, colluvial mixing, and the varying mobility of surface material. In the foreground, shrubs cover the level surface of the red beds, but vegetation establishes itself with difficulty on the loose, porous scree slopes.

A Systems Approach

The definition and examination of systems, more or less simplified for study purposes, enables the complexities of the real, observed world to be considered in an orderly manner. We can see more clearly the interrelationships between the components of a system and the flows of energy and matter which take place within it—even though, as page 43 shows, field measurements and analysis may be required to establish causal relationships between vegetation forms and environmental variables. We simplify to see how the system is structured and to consider how the components may be further studied and measured. Simplifications involve subjective actions. We need to define the limits of study and to specify the systems and subsystems themselves.

We are concerned with ecosystems and with human socio-economic systems and their interactions. Matter and energy continuously pass through a mature ecosystem; but within it the complex plant and animal organisms and the elements of their habitat are approximately in a state of equilibrium. Here we are dealing with savanna lands, where it is acknowledged that the areal distribution of what may broadly be defined as 'savanna vegetation' depends to a considerable extent on human actions, past and present. Most economic systems involving man are extremely complex; but a systems approach enables us initially to isolate human components and consider, in turn, other relevant variables of the atmosphere, lithosphere and biosphere.

The supply of nutrients to plants involves fundamental, vital processes. So, in examining our particular savanna areas, we concentrate on soil systems and their relationships with vegetation systems. First, however, we must establish what is meant by 'savanna' and observe the composition and location of different forms of savanna vegetation—that is, the plant associations which make up these various forms and their habitats. It is usually difficult to determine which of the many variables acting on plant life result in savanna vegetation rather than scrubland or forest, or produce a particular type of savanna. It would appear that the dominant variables differ from place to place and that combinations of external influences are often very significant. Therefore we must examine in detail the components of various systems and subsystems to identify the more important relationships in the broad environmental system.

Finally, and hopefully with a clear understanding of interrelationships, we consider particular areas of savanna in various parts of the world and we look at their own unique, complex integrated systems.

The Vegetation-Soil System

In this particular kind of ecosystem, a savanna, no physical or biotic factor operates in complete independence: everything within it is related to everything else to some degree, and there are a large number of variables. Our aim is to identify the most important relationships *within* the system and the extent to which particular external variables control these relationships. We are looking, in fact, at a kind of supersystem. Within this we identify a plant system and a soil system. Their interrelationships are obviously of prime importance. Between them there are transfers of energy and materials, and plant productivity depends largely on soil nutrient inputs. It is therefore desirable to study the interaction of key components which affect the available nutrient store in the soil.

First we set our own limits to the open system, in this case a form of savanna vegetation in a particular, defined location. Figs. 1 and 2 show such an open system and the exchanges of energy and matter with its environment which are needed for its maintenance and preservation. It may reach a state where its properties appear almost constant over a long period—approaching a steady-state equilibrium.

The chosen internal component systems are those of plants and soil. Climatic elements are seen as among the external independent variables affecting them. There are certain universal climatic influences on the world's tropical grasslands: for example, a high solar radiant input is

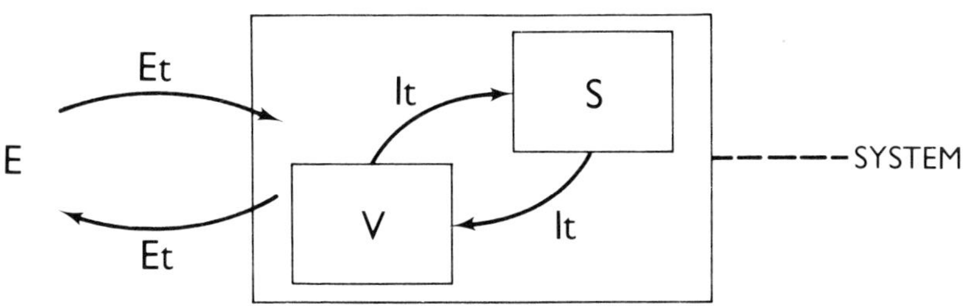

Transfers of energy/mass t

Control variables: External E; Internal I

Sub-system

V Vegetation

S Soil

Fig. 1 Internal transfers are shown between the soil and vegetation systems: examples are the flows involved in nutrient cycling. External transfers involve nutrient inputs from rocks or the atmosphere, and the solar energy inputs which affect both soils and plants.

characteristic of tropical ecosytems and the net radiation values (incoming minus outgoing radiation) are high throughout the year. Temperatures and net radiation are thus generally adequate for plant growth. However, evapo-transpiration rates are also apt to be high, and so the limiting climatic factor for plant growth is likely to be the precipitation, and its seasonal distribution and intensity are of great importance. But climate controls internal variables, such as the rate of weathering of rocks and the release of soil nutrients; so that we must consider local climatic influences affecting the inputs and losses of nutrients through weathering and leaching (Fig. 2).

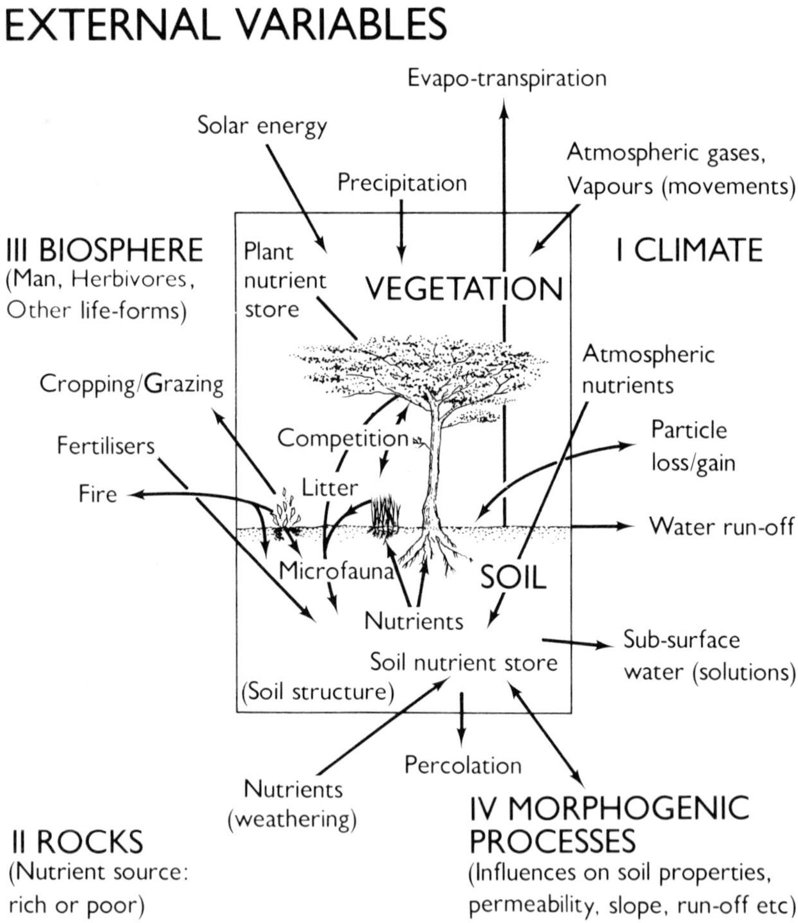

Fig. 2 These four broad categories of external variables affecting the savanna soil-vegetation system are considered separately in the book. For instance, changes in the state of the system with time, resulting from matter and energy transfers, lead us to examine: I effects of climatic fluctuations; II depletion of mineral resources; III over-cultivation; IV duricrust formation.

We look in turn at other variables affecting the working of this internal plant-soil system which is under primary consideration. These, for study purposes, are seen as part of the surrounding environment. Among them are the rock types (lithological features) and the biotic variables, including man and the various herbivores, wild or domesticated, whose cropping, grazing, manuring etc. effect transfers across the system boundaries.

The Availability and Storage of Nutrients

Ninety-five per cent of the dry weight of protoplasm in plants is made up of the atmospheric elements carbon, hydrogen, oxygen and nitrogen, though over forty other elements are needed by most living organisms. The chemical weathering of rocks and soil particles make such elements available for plant nourishment. Calcium, magnesium, potassium, sodium, phosphorus, sulphur, silicon, iron and aluminium, are widely available—though a soil may lack a particular element. Weathering releases other elements which plants require in very small amounts, but which are vital to their development, such as manganese, zinc, cobalt and copper.

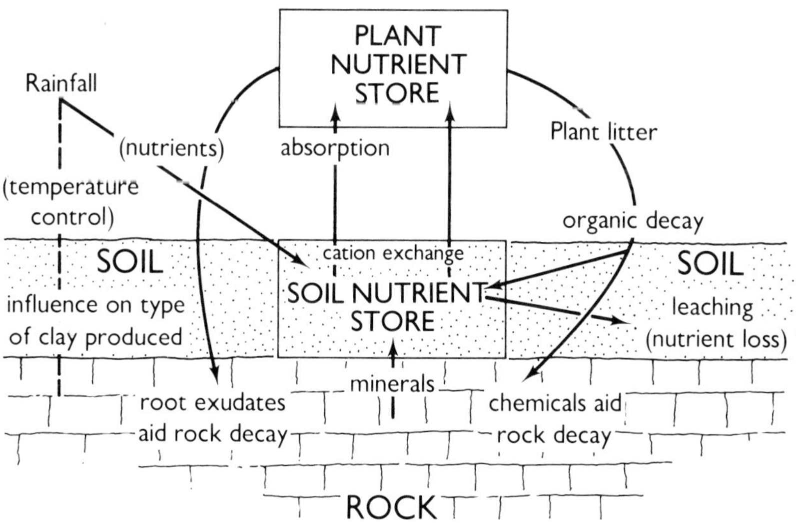

Fig. 3 A simple diagram which focuses attention on interactions which are in themselves complex. For example, nutrients derived from rocks promote strong plant growth, while chemicals exuded from plant roots may accelerate rock weathering and liberate more nutrients. Acids from decaying plant litter can affect the rate of breakdown of clays. Some plants produce and exude chemicals which inhibit the growth of competitive plants, or even their own seedlings, so ensuring a satisfactory intake of moisture and nutrients.

Very soluble soil compounds are available for absorption by plants, but are apt to be lost from the soil by leaching. However, tiny clay particles in association with humus (as a clay-humus complex) can firmly retain vital metal ions (cations). These cations may pass into the plants in exchange for hydrogen ions released from rootlets.

The nutrients received in solution are temporarily 'stored' in plants, together with the elements received from photosynthetic and nitrifying processes. When plant litter decomposes, it releases these into the soil, and provides organic acids which may aid rock weathering. These cycling processes are shown in Fig. 3.

In savanna lands the amount of soil water and its ability to support plants vary as wet and dry seasons alternate. Even in the wet season, the field capacity of a soil—when water just fills the smaller soil spaces—may only be achieved intermittently; though in short dry spells soil solutions, in the form of thick films, may still move up through soil spaces by capillary action and become readily available to plants. But during the dry season, plant absorption and evapo-transpiration reduce the soil water content, until there may not be sufficient to prevent the plants from wilting. Water may be present, but unavailable, for a thin film adheres strongly to soil particles. The proportion of water at this point is the permanent wilting percentage (Fig. 4).

Other factors affect the mass of nutrients in particular parts of the plant-soil system, and thus the development of the vegetation. A rock weathers and supplies nutrients. As these are removed and transferred through the various cycles, or are lost to the system through drainage or percolation, there is an increase in weathering potential. The rock continues to supply nutrients, though the continued supply depends on

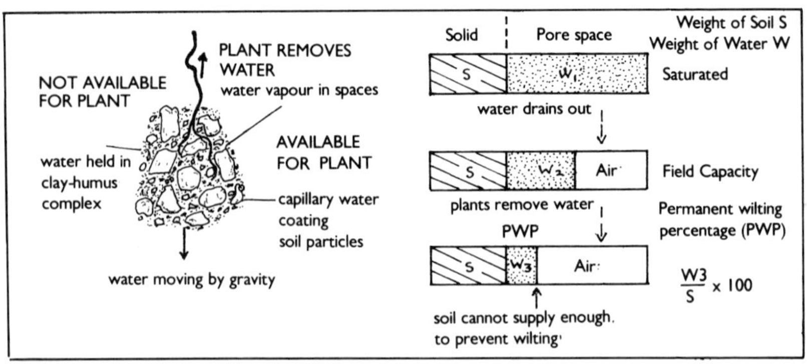

Fig. 4 Gravitational pull, cohesive forces, capillary action, and evaporation all act to allow water and solutions to move through the soil, and govern the proportions of solid matter, liquids, gases, and vapours. The bar graphs show such proportions under conditions of waterlogging, field capacity, and wilting.

the rock itself: mineral sources can eventually become depleted. Sometimes the loss can be too rapid; for example, if a large proportion of nutrients is retained in the plants, the removal of the vegetation will mean a drastic loss to the system. Nutrients might be slowly replaced by weathering (or by adding manure or artificial fertiliser to restore the balance). On the other hand, if the weathering products, with their potential nutrient supply, are not taken into the plant-soil system, nor removed from the system by physical processes, and so accumulate, they tend to slow down weathering processes.

Savanna—Composition and Distribution

The term 'savanna' is generally used to describe tropical grasslands. They range from virtually treeless grassland to those with a close, but discontinuous, cover of drought-resistant trees or shrubs. But there is a diversity of composition, and of plant form and habitat.

By definition, the tropical savannas have a dominant herbaceous stratum. This is made up of perennial grasses and sedges, usually with xerophytic characteristics—adapted to periodic droughts. Most of the grasses have a tussock habit. As in other forms of vegetation, there are various communities containing plants with different life forms. Each of these may be represented by a different species: for example, the many trees of the African tall-grass savanna which shed their leaves in the dry season include numerous species of *Acacia*, *Combretum*, and *Brachystegia*, each with their characteristic shapes and heights. The Australian savannas include a very great number of species of evergreen *Eucalyptus*; while numerous species of palm are common in the South American savannas.

The world's savannas are often associated with the extensive surfaces of little relief which occur within and just outside the tropics. They cover huge areas of plains and tablelands. The boundaries of these areas are shown boldly enough in Fig. 5, but, in fact, it is often difficult to decide where the limits really are. Most savannas appear to be located in areas lying between tropical rainforest and semi-arid forms of vegetation; but, even where this is so, they may shade gradually into these bounding types of vegetation, and often contain within them smaller areas of untypical plant associations of varying density. Such internal variations are to be expected in view of the innumerable interacting factors which affect plant communities. Think of the complex interactions within a *physical environment* which embodies a variety of rock types, macro- and micro-climates, localised water sources, active geomorphic processes, and soil variations. Consider the *biotic influences*, which include the effects of other plants and micro-organisms as well as animals, and the human activities (*anthropogenic factors*) which create agricultural areas,

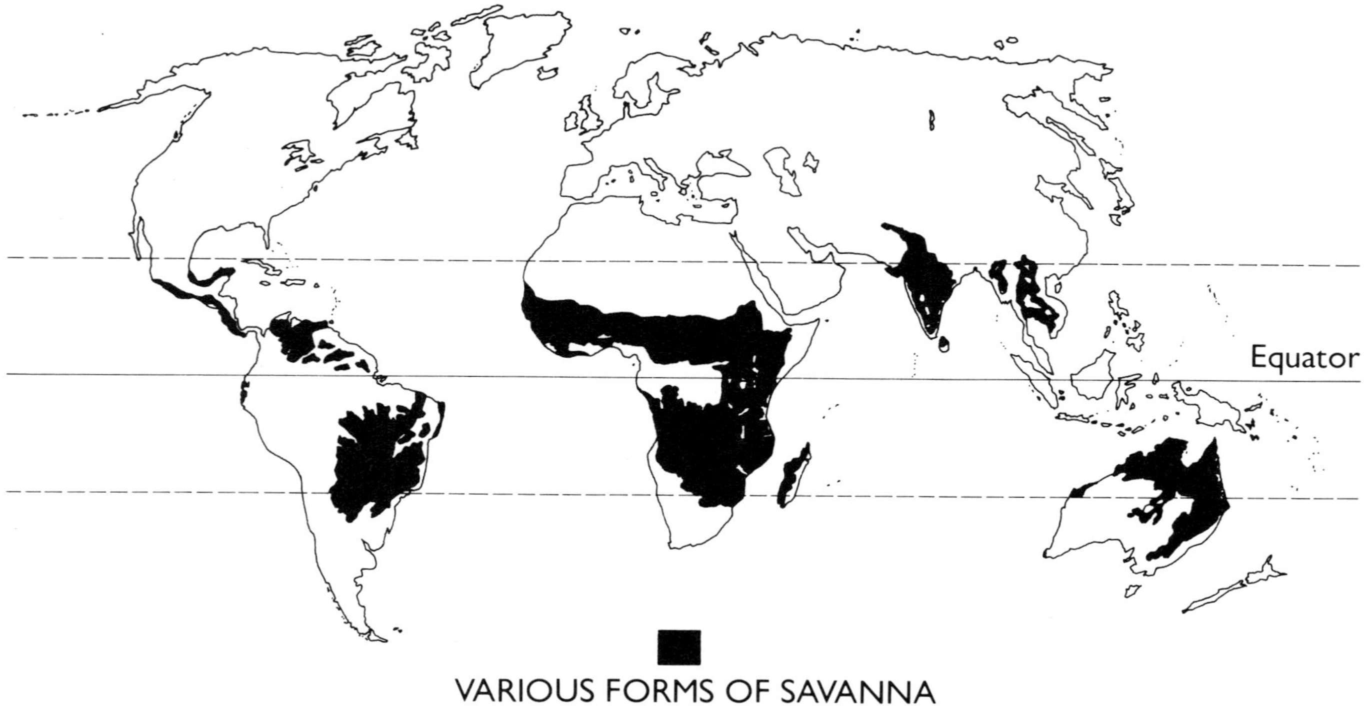

Fig. 5 The distribution of the world's savannas. Notice the extent to which savanna covers tropical tablelands in South America, Africa, India and Australia. Such a map masks the variety of plant associations within the areas shown and cannot, of course, indicate dominant causes, whether climatic, edaphic, or anthropogenic.

introduce domestic animals, develop settlements, and interfere with water distribution.

Most of these influential factors are apt to change, and at varying rates. Any savanna area experiences large fluctuations of energy and matter with the passage of time. On a relatively short time-scale, plant species respond to diurnal changes in available solar radiation and to changing atmospheric conditions. Changes of size, form and habit during the life-cycles of plants and animals are also strong biotic influences. Physical changes, such as sporadic volcanic activity or disturbances by a termite colony, can affect soil mineral content and cause striking contrasts in plant associations.

The Location and Extent of Savannas

The location between tropical rainforest and semi-desert[1] would suggest a gradual change in the nature of the vegetation from tall-grass woodland savanna to dry grassland with a few woody trees or xerophytic shrubs, in response to decreasing annual rainfall, fewer rainy months during the year, and increasingly long periods of drought. Yet in many tropical lands there is little correlation between the amount and duration of precipitation and the occurrence of savanna. In moist areas, which seemingly should support forest, we may find treeless savanna alternating with stretches of woodland. In central Nigeria, for instance, areas of tall-grass savanna with low trees are intermingled with close dry woodland, and in places there is tropical rainforest. In more arid environments large stretches of dry grassland with woody shrubs alternate with xerophytic scrub, as in north-western Australia.

However, most of the broad continental areas of savanna do have marked seasonal droughts, when evapo-transpiration rates are high. There is usually a permanent water deficit below two or three metres, though the moisture in the upper parts of the regolith and soil may be sufficient to support a form of savanna. Under these conditions the herbaceous plants which complete a rapid life-cycle, and have shallow spreading root systems, appear to have advantages over trees and shrubs.

Despite the local variations, it is possible to recognise major categories within savanna formations over large regional areas. Pages 34 and 38 discuss characteristics of various parts of the South American and Australian savannas. In East and Central Africa, much of the ancient pediplains of Zambia and Tanzania bear savanna woodlands, frequently referred to as *miombo*. This comprises various associations with the *Brachystegia, Isoberlina* and *Julbernadia* tree species. These deep-rooted trees are slow growing, taking some 60–70 years to reach maturity, when their trunk size is about 400 millimetres in diameter. Their leaves appear just before the rainy season and are shed in the middle part of the dry

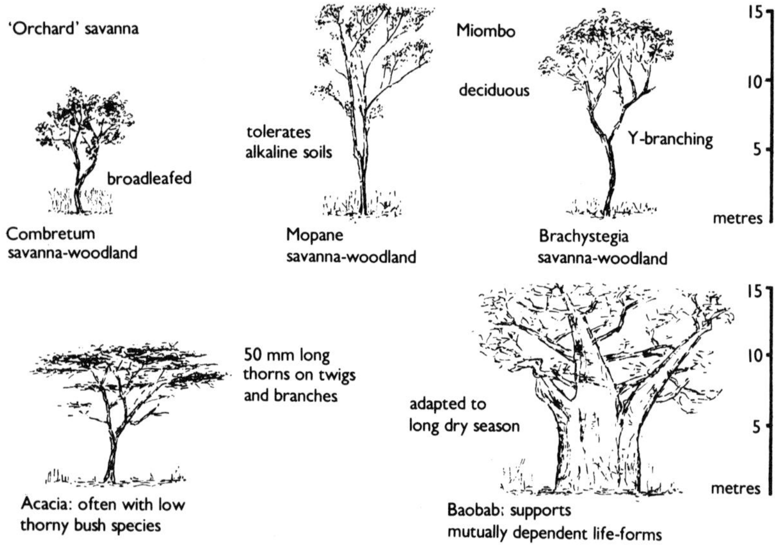

Fig. 6 Very broadly, the trees shown at the top are often dominant in close woodland tall-grass savanna, depending on soil conditions. The *Acacia* illustrated is more frequently found in drier conditions, often associated with open grassy 'parkland' savanna. The baobab, adapted to withstand drought, is a complex environmental system in itself, acting as host to numerous mutually dependant micro- and macro-organisms.

season. In dry locations the associated plants are mainly short grasses; in wetter parts the grass cover is more luxuriant, with shrubs and small trees in the understorey.

Elsewhere in East Africa there are expanses of open grassland, and huge areas of 'parkland' with species of *Acacia* and *Terminalia*, and stretches of thorny scrub with close *Acacia*. Many moister parts have medium-sized, broad leaved trees, mostly of the *Combretum* species, scattered in an 'orchard' savanna. Despite their extent, the causes of these particular savanna associations are debatable, as we shall see (page 14). Space forbids reference to many tree species adapted to particular ecological circumstances, but exception must be made for the baobab. The very slow growing African baobab is adapted to places with soil water deficiencies. Its trunk, often over ten metres in diameter, and the lower parts of its branches can store large amounts of water. Transpiration losses are reduced by the short time it bears leaves, usually for several weeks. The baobab and various *Acacia* species also occur widely in the West African savannas, which also have a characteristic tree, the shea (*Butyrospermum parkii*), from whose oily seeds the edible fat, shea butter, is obtained.

Fig. 7 Dry parkland savanna with *Acacia*, in southern Kenya, with a rhinoceros in the foreground and elephants on the hillside. The grasses also support huge herds of migrating zebra and wildebeeste.

Fig. 8 *Terminalia* occupying red-brown loams on limestone country in Zambia, south of Lusaka. The presence of a lighter species of grass in the foreground is a response to a low termite mound.[3]

The floristic composition of savannas is often revealing. It may indicate that present areas of tropical grassland once bore rainforest. This seems to be the case both in the grasslands in Brazil and Guyana bordering the Amazonian rainforests, and in isolated savanna patches deep within the forests of Zaïre. In parts of West Africa, *separate* savanna areas possess similar floristic composition quite distinct from the forests which enclose them. This suggests a much more extensive savanna covering in the past, during a period of more general aridity. In fact, during the drier inter-pluvials of the Pleistocene, closed forest seems to have been very restricted.

Because of the great diversity of composition, form, and habitat of the savannas, it is difficult to make any valid generalisation about the reason for their nature and distribution. Among the causes might be:

1 Present climatic conditions: especially the occurrence of regular seasonal droughts.
2 The availability, or otherwise, of various soil nutrients (which would reflect the influences of present and past climatic conditions on soil structure and mineral content).
3 Drainage conditions, affected by relief and the permeability, or otherwise, of soil and regolith.
4 Past climatic influences which favoured a widespread savanna vegetation, so that the now separated stretches of savanna may be relict areas.
5 Periodic fires, which prevent the regeneration of plants which otherwise might form close woodland. A high proportion of savanna plants are pyrophytes. A fire climax form of vegetation may reflect exposure to fires during the dry season.
6 Grazing by herbivores, which may also prevent the development of plants beyond the seedling stage, and check woodland regeneration. The trampling may also affect soil structure and the availability of nutrients.

These varied and often influential factors are expressed in the broadest terms, but give some idea of the need for a detailed systematic study of the particular area of savanna under investigation.

External Variables
I Climatic Influences

The Effects of Wet/Dry Seasons on Soil Conditions

Savanna is most often associated with tropical areas which have a wet season followed by a period of drought. Fig. 9 shows the rainfall regimes of six places in the savanna lands shown on page 10. Sholapur and

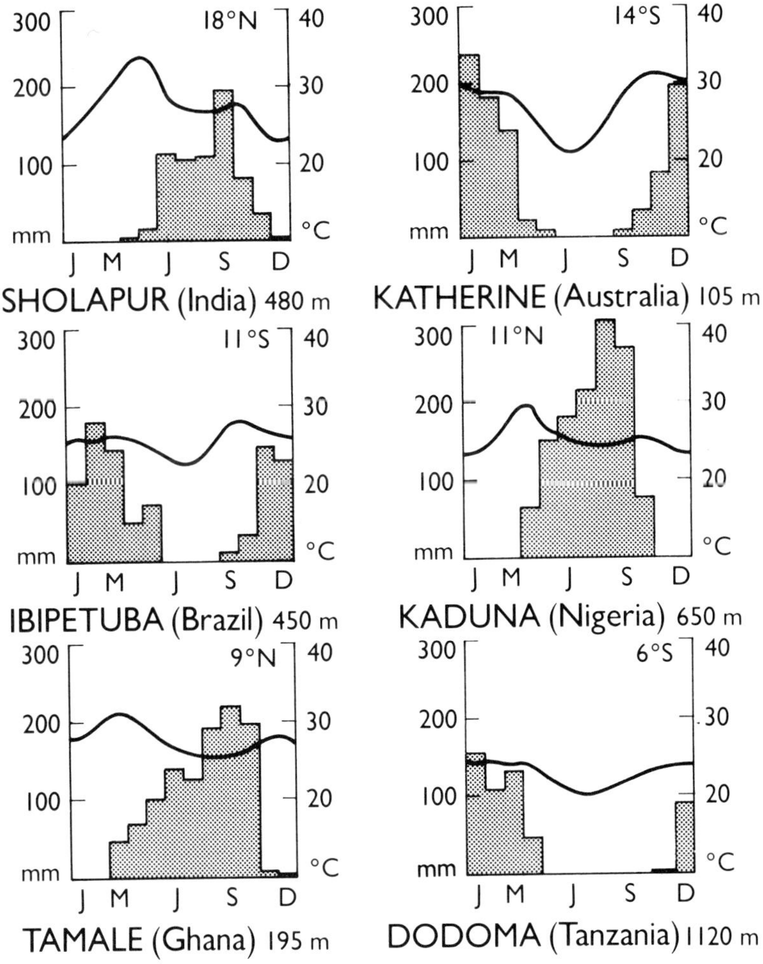

Fig. 9 Mean monthly rainfall and temperature for six selected places in a savanna environment. Heights above sea-level are shown in metres.

Katherine are affected in summer by a monsoonal inflow of moist air; the others by rainfall with heavy storms associated with instability in an inter-tropical zone of convergence.

The mean figures for Kaduna show the marked wet and dry seasons, and that temperatures fall slightly in the wet months, due to the cloud cover. The daily maximum is mostly about 35–38°C throughout the year. The mean relative humidity is as low as 14 per cent at 1530 hrs in January, but over 70 per cent in July and August, when 50–100 mm of rain may fall in a day.

In the humid tropics the combination of high temperatures and moist conditions favours the decomposition of complex silicates in the rocks and soil particles. In wet conditions soluble bases are lost by leaching and drainage, and liberated silica, aluminium, and iron hydroxides move downward in the soil, which has a clayey texture. Weathering tends to produce a deep red, clayey regolith. In undisturbed forest the decomposition of litter makes nutrients available to plants. But, by contrast with the upper soil, the lower parts tend to be impoverished by leaching, and contain inert matter; though minerals liberated by the weathering bedrock may counteract this.

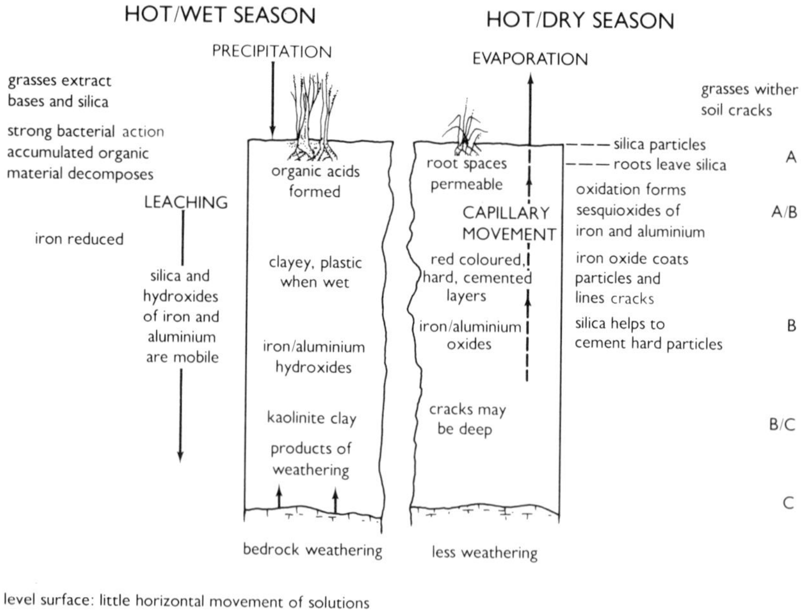

Fig. 10 Generalised soil profiles, showing processes during wet and dry seasons under savanna grassland.

Under alternating wet and dry conditions the results are rather different. Less organic matter is returned to the soil, and the effects of the rainfall vary as the wet season progresses. During the wettest period organic acids and soil solutions can move downwards and promote chemical decomposition of the bedrock, and, of course, produce mobile iron and aluminium hydroxides. There is not the strong, continuous leaching that occurs in perennially humid climates. Beneath level surfaces lack of horizontal movement allows accumulation in the B zone. As conditions become drier, the less abundant soil water has a higher concentration of bases. The rates of weathering of the bedrock and decomposition of the silicates slow down. As the soils dry out they crack; holes are also left by root decay and insect activity, allowing air to oxidise the hydroxides to stable, less mobile sesquioxides. Hard lumps coated with crystalline iron oxide may become cemented. Silica, which goes into solution in the wet periods, tends to combine with iron to precipitate ferruginous quartzite. As a result, a hardened zone (a *duricrust*, or *cuirasse*) may form, with iron and aluminium compounds making up a large part of the concreted mass; however, the accretions may be in nodular form, and the mass only partly concreted.

The savanna grasses, with a dense, shallow root system, obtain most of their mineral nutrients during the wet season. They extract silica, and have a much higher concentration of silica than other plants. When they die and decompose much of the silica is left on and in the soil. The minute particles, more soluble than primary silicates, form part of the cyclic system seen in Fig. 11.

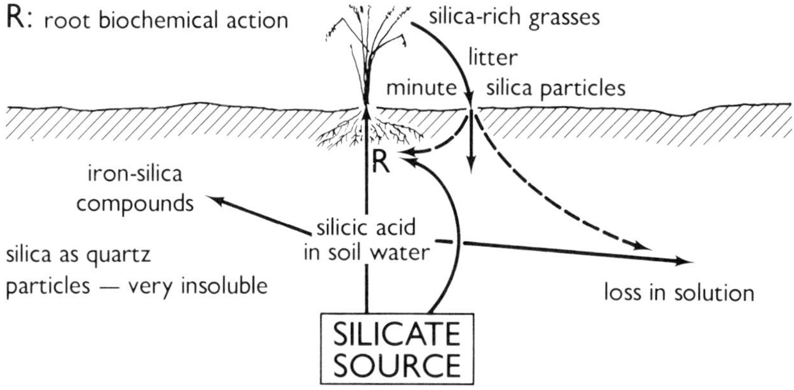

Fig. 11 Some of the processes involved in silica cycling in the tropical savannas.

There are also other herbs with tubers or bulbs, which enable them to come rapidly into leaf and flower during the rainy season; they, too, find nutrients close to the surface. But most of the trees and shrubs of the savannas have long roots, which enable them to obtain water and nutrients, when available, from greater depths.

The exact balance between grasses, trees and shrubs may thus be affected by the development of hardened zones in permeable soils under tropical wet and dry conditions, as well as by the minerals available from a particular rock, by the angle of slope, and by the effects of agents which act to disturb the soil, such as termite activity, or fire which may increase near-surface hardness.

Permeability and Soil Development

The permeability of soils varies with the seasons, with consequent effects on surface run-off. The first violent showers of the rainy season fall on a hardened surface, which may or may not be deeply cracked. Deciduous vegetation offers little protection at this time, and there are few annuals growing between the perennial grass tussocks. Sheets of water run across the surface until they infiltrate the more permeable rocks or else evaporate. As the grasses and shrubs grow leaves, the screening effect of the vegetation increases, for the plants absorb water, and interception by foliage is greater, so the overland flow tends to decrease. As the season progresses the soil water content increases.

The permeability of rocks and regoliths influences soil development and vegetation forms. A fine textured clayey regolith is less likely to develop a duricrust. Nevertheless, its complex silicate molecules still break down in the wet season and the minute clay particles attract and retain mobile iron compounds. On dessication, cracks and old root spaces may become lined with small iron concretions, and quartz grains become coated with iron oxide. As a result, the now red-coloured clay may tend to become less plastic.

Grasses and trees tend to be direct competitors for water, particularly at the end of the dry season, and the dense rooting system of grasses is in their favour on fine textured soils in the drier locations. Where the annual rainfall is less than 250 mm, such soils often support open grassland. Woody plants stand a better chance as the rainfall increases, especially on stonier soils, where their long deep roots can exploit deep resources. On the other hand, deep sandy soils may allow water to infiltrate too rapidly and make woodland less likely. It is revealing that on sandy terrain the presence of clay lenses is often indicated by their accompanying tree clusters amid a savanna grassland.

On lowlands, such as the Llanos of Venezuela, where floods alternate with a period with low water-table, sandy sediments become waterlogged during the rainy season, which inhibits bacterial activity and also oxidation—preventing the release of nutrients. During the dry season the water-table may be very low. Tree growth is therefore excluded; yet sedges, mosses and other marsh plants occur, as well as grasses, in what is sometimes called a 'water savanna'. Sometimes hard layers may develop under such conditions. The water-saturated anaerobic environment favours the accumulation of organic compounds and reduction to ferrous iron; but during the dry season oxidation produces insoluble ferric compounds which build up a hard layer in the zone of the fluctuating water-table.

The composition and distribution of particular types of rock can, therefore, produce a corresponding variety of plant–soil systems. It is thus appropriate at this point to look at the influence of certain categories of rock formations within the lands shown in Fig. 5.

II The Influences of Local Rocks

One of the advantages of a systems approach is that while primarily considering the effects of certain control variables, such as the climatic ones, on parts of a system, other variables may be seen to be involved—bedrock weathering which provides nutrients, for example—but these particular influences can be set aside for detailed examination later. We have already seen the significance of rock weathering, and can now turn to specific cases.

Although most rock types respond rather similarly to the tropical wet and dry seasonal conditions, there are variations; for example, the tendency of clays to promote flocculation rather than layering, and the way that layering may occur in some very porous rocks. Yet tendencies remain; and even pure sands, initially lacking iron oxides, may, from dust or solutions, acquire iron oxides and chemical coatings on their grains. Their voids may become filled, and in some cases concretions formed, producing a red-coloured aggregate which retains more water. The nature of the savanna vegetation changes accordingly, for the xerophytes now meet competition from mesophytic species.

The wet season weathering of various igneous rocks results in characteristic regoliths, soils, and forms of vegetation. Basic igneous rocks, rich in ferromagnesian minerals and poor in quartz, produce much iron-rich clay, forming a dark regolith with a slow rate of infiltration. This encourages overland flow, so that during drought the upper parts of soil remain particularly dry. This and the soil basicity favour grasses rather than shrubs and trees. Solutions flowing from such rocks onto lowlands or into depressions may create iron-rich horizons and encourage duricrust formation in their soils (page 32).

In those parts of tropical and sub-tropical Australia, the Indian Deccan, north-east Uganda, and Ethiopia, where basic igneous rocks weather under wet and dry seasonal conditions, the clays produced tend to shrink and develop deep, wide cracks during drought. The cracks may extend downwards for a metre or so and engulf surface materials falling into them. These may remain trapped when, later, the clays become wet and swell. Such expansions and contractions can produce a slow churning of the soil. Alkaline 'vertisols' may result, often very dark; those derived from calcium-rich igneous rocks may develop a horizon of calcium carbonate at the depth of maximum penetration of the cracks. Grassland savanna covers most of these soils, even where some have initially been covered by forest.

The regolith developed on acid igneous rocks is often deep, with a

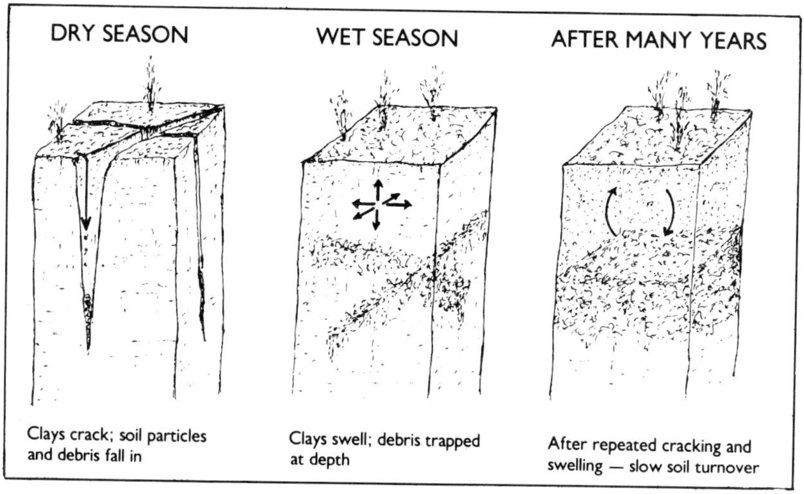

Fig. 12 Vertisol formation, with surface material transferred to lower levels. Alternating contractions and swellings can cause either layering at depth or a slow vertical exchange of material.

high proportion of quartz sand, and thus has a tendency to be readily permeable. In especially wet locations, bases are leached from the weathering rock during the rainy season and kaolin clay is formed. Here, in acidic conditions, as the bases are leached out the silica is less likely to go into solution. There is less tendency to form cuirasses and the vegetation responds accordingly, as seen in Fig. 21.

Quite apart from their ability to provide soil nutrients, by virtue of their chemical composition, rocks must be able to retain sufficient water to make the minerals available in soil solutions, and so rock structure is important. But near-surface rock formations are not necessarily uniform, and structure may vary with depth, and so affect plant cover.

In quite dry parts of South-West Africa, for instance, layered sandstones support stretches of shrub savanna. The porous upper stratum allows water to seep through. During rainy periods, grasses rooted in the porous material absorb sufficient water for growth and during the dry season the aerial leaves and shoot system die: the root system and terminal growth-point of the shoot, well-protected, survive. More consolidated, jointed sandstones lie 20–30 cm beneath. Water seeps into the joints and is available for shrubs rooted in the cracks. Together, the grasses and bushes, positioned according to the underlying cracks, form a shrub savanna, neither plant form competing with the other.

III The Biosphere—a Variety of Influences

Apart from the internal actions of soil micro-organisms, a vast number of external variables affecting plant-soil systems form part of the general biosphere. Their activities can greatly modify the flow processes which take place within the systems. Here we look at the effects of insects and larger animals, and especially at the disturbances created by man. Fires are also considered here, for although many savanna fires have natural causes, such as lightning, the majority are caused by man, deliberately or accidentally.

Termite Activity

In building their mounds termites may bring up three or four cubic metres of fine clayey material and sand grains from deep in the soil. Mixed with saliva and dejecta, these may become stabilised and form a resistant mass, until eventually abandoned by the colony. Many savanna

Fig. 13 An *Acacia* in the savanna of northern Tanzania, with new weaver birds' nests at the extremities of its branches, where there is less danger from snakes. The latter often occupy cracks and holes in old termitaries, as in the termite mound to the left.

areas have closely spaced mounds, three or four metres high, so that the amount of mixing of soil material is great. It is difficult to establish precise relationships between their occurrences and the nature of the underlying rock, but silt or clay is needed for construction, with a certain humidity of soil and atmosphere, and local food resources. Termites help the decomposition and recycling of organic matter.

They can bring up sand and clay through the openings in moderately thick duricrusts, and even cause subsidence and breaking of the hard layers. Plants finding the new environment favourable may spread roots and also help to break the crusts. Woody trees and shrubs are frequently seen growing on old termitaries amid otherwise grassy savannas.

Fire and Its Effects

People have long used slash-and-burn techniques to clear the land, and hunters have started fires to flush animals. Even settled communities start fires to clear litter and promote new growth. The effects are varied and complex.[2] The temperature of the surface under a grass fire is high, and even higher under bush and tree fires. This parches the soil, bakes the clays, and dehydrates iron oxides. When surface temperatures rise to 200–300°C, at a metre's depth it may still be over 60°C. Surface baking can diminish the permeability of a soil and increase overland flow, although some clayey topsoils become crumbly.

Mineral nutrients retained in the plants are released by fire, and those which are not blown or washed away may return to the soil. Fire can cause chemical changes, and may even produce soluble compounds of nitrogen and other elements not otherwise available to the plants. This may increase soil fertility, aid plant regeneration, and perhaps allow colonisation by new species.

On the other hand, the destruction of many of the plants and associated animal communities by fire can promote ecological instability. Recurrent fires may eliminate susceptible plants, while those better adapted may survive and come to dominate the vegetation. The Australian tea-tree only releases its seeds after a sufficiently high temperature is reached: it has become dominant over large areas of bush and woodland savanna where fires are frequent. However, many Australian eucalypts are fire tolerant.

Where successive fires occur, invading fire-resistant species of tree and shrub are more likely to become established. It seems probable that after fierce burning many areas formerly covered by deciduous or semi-evergreen forest, with dense undergrowth, have been succeeded by forms of savanna with fire-resistant woody species. Some feel that a large proportion of the world's savannas are mainly fire climax communities. On the whole, grasses and perennial herbs are better adapted to withstand the effects of fires than are trees and shrubs. Some grasses, like the African forage grass *Themeda triandra*, have seeds whose germination is encouraged by fire.

Once forest cover has been replaced by a form of savanna, grazing by wild herbivores or man's herds removes young shoots and may thus prevent the regeneration of woody plants. The grass family is best equipped to withstand grazing and trampling, and grass growth, with a rapid production of new shoots, may be stimulated by such treatment, and also by light burning. However, as Fig. 14 indicates, excessive grazing and over-burning may inhibit recovery and lead to surface erosion. Support for the idea that large areas of savanna have fire climax communities maintained by firing and grazing comes from northern Tanzania and north-western Nigeria, where parts of the savanna have been protected from fire and grazing for long periods. In each case the proportion of woody plants has greatly increased. It is unlikely, of course, that a cleared forest area would thus regain its former climax balance of plants. The alteration in soil structure alone would influence the sequence of colonisation by shrubs and trees.

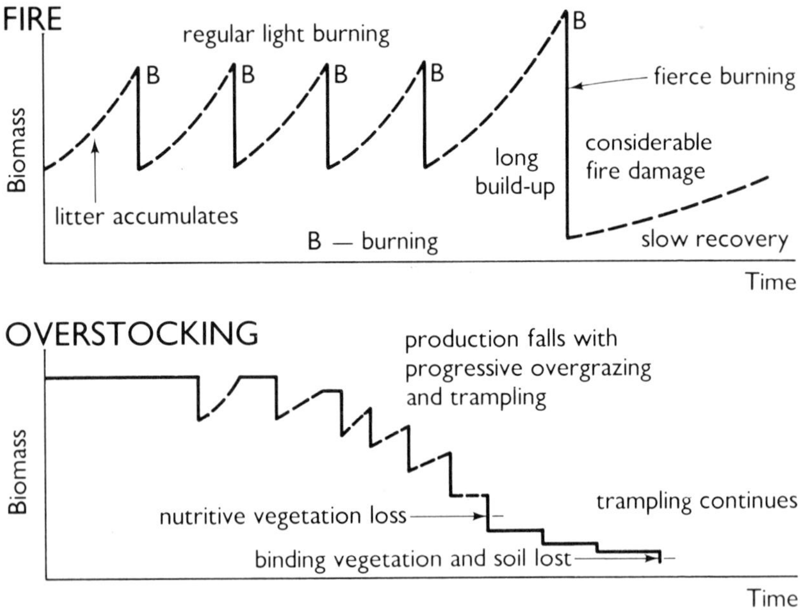

Fig. 14 The upper graph shows that, in an area of tree savanna, light burning at short intervals may allow the biomass to build up to roughly the same amount as before. But an occasional fire after a longer period of litter accumulation may so damage the vegetation that recovery and build-up are slow. The lower graph shows that, with progressive removal of nutrients and interference with soil texture, a time is reached when vegetation does not recover, leading finally to the loss of unprotected soil.

Man's Pastoral and Agricultural Activities

Overgrazing, over-burning, and the use of cropping systems which fail to return sufficient nutrients all have serious effects on savannas with fragile tropical soils. Normally the plants themselves check surface flow and help to prevent sheet erosion and concentration which would lead to gully formation. Obviously savanna vegetation is not as effective as forest cover in these respects, and effectiveness varies in the cases of high grass–tree savanna and sparse tussock grassland with thorn-bush. But any destruction of natural vegetation, even in the savannas, removes plants which check flow and directly protect the soil against splash erosion.

Semi-nomadic activities based on the movement of cattle, in response to seasonal changes in the conditions of the grasslands, have been typical of tribal groups on the African savannas—such as the Fulani on the dry grasslands of West Africa, and the Maasai in East Africa. A natural balance had been achieved between men, their animals, their temporary settlements, and land-use related to local climate and vegetation. Now pressures of population and government controls are tending to restrict such movements; consequently there has been increasing settlement and overstocking in the somewhat more humid parts.

Closer tribal settlement has long existed in savanna lands. But in less populous times soil deterioration could be countered by local migration. This used to be typical of the West African grasslands lying to the south of the Sahel. Here, with some 500 mm of rain a year, the soils, subjected to only moderate leaching, acquired a satisfactory organic content and supply of bases, and in many places calcium salts gave a good crumb structure. A typical village, with vegetable gardens close to the huts, would have had about it a ring of open fields for food crops. Year after year, millet, the most common crop, would have been planted in May and harvested in August. Some manure might have been added during the fallow months, but usually very little. The fields beyond this usually would have had no manuring, but would have grown either millet or a cash crop, such as groundnuts. These would have been left for a few years after the harvest, but perhaps grazed or burnt over. The unreliability of the rainfall added to the precariousness of such arrangements. But as fertility dropped, and the rings of land became sterile, the community would have migrated and settled elsewhere. Today, however, the people have become more static, and natural increase and in-migration have added to the problems of the Sahel.

Surprisingly, perhaps, the tree savanna to the south of this, in the bettered watered areas of West Africa, has proved particularly hazardous for settlement in the long term. Here the greater leaching has produced iron-rich illuviated layers. The organic matter and bases available in the upper parts of the soil are soon depleted by the forms of land-use

Fig. 15 This country near Enugu in Nigeria (just over 6°N) receives over 1800 mm of rain a year, and has a relatively short dry period, between November and February. Yet only a few areas, like that within the far loop of the river, are covered with thick woodland. The most regularly cultivated areas are the river flats below the well-defined terrace edges. Elsewhere the landscape is a patchwork of cultivated fields and abandoned plots covered with grasses, shrubs and scattered trees.

described above. Burning, as we have seen, can lead to an unstable soil structure, so that erosion may expose a hard pan, leaving an infertile zone about the settlement; a disastrous situation where migration is not possible.

Rotational bush felling on the more fertile soils under woodland savanna involves clearing and burning. A short fallow period may follow six to ten years' cultivation before, finally, the land is abandoned. Among the savanna woodlands of central Africa a type of shifting cultivation known as *chitamene* is practised. A small patch selected for cultivation is cleared and covered with piles of branches from the trees and shrubs of the surrounding miombo. These are burnt just before the first rains and seeds planted in the ash. This is not wholly advantageous. Soil bacteria may suffer, nitrogen compounds may be lost with the smoke, and soluble potassium salts leached away. After about three years' cultivation the land is abandoned. Obviously this affects an area possibly three times greater than the third of a hectare or so actually cultivated. When left, after some thirty years the patch may revert to a form of

Fig. 16 Cattle crossing savanna in northern Tanzania, where a combination of overgrazing and trampling by large numbers of wild herbivores has reduced vegetation to the bare dusty condition you see here. Yet, in the distance, a line of trees follows the course of a seasonal stream.

woodland savanna, though the plant composition will vary from the original. In practice, abandoned land may be re-occupied before this, so that a form of grassy tree savanna comes to be a more common association in a landscape which is a patchwork of modified vegetation forms. The pollarded trees outside the cultivated patch continue to grow, unless incidentally damaged by fire.

Within the broad belts of savanna, some areas of exceptional fertility, with assured water supplies, have become districts of close population; for instance, the country to the north of Lake Victoria (p. 36). Elsewhere, European colonisation of potentially fertile savanna land has increased food production and introduced plantation crops, such as sisal in northern Tanzania and tobacco in Zimbabwe (Rhodesia). Investment and technical innovations in cultivation, water supply, transport and communications made this possible. But the fragile balance, so easily disturbed by cultivation, is emphasised by such notable failures as the mechanically assisted groundnut farming at Kongwa in Tanzania, begun in the late 1940s. Huge investment could not make up for hasty assessments. Conditions appeared favourable: the average rainfall of 500 mm appeared suitable for cropping, while the relative aridity of the savannas was unfavourable to the tsetse fly which affects men and ungulates in moister bush country. But the fluctuations in rainfall, from 150 to 625 mm per annum while the scheme operated, proved otherwise. The deep-rooted bush was difficult to clear, and the disc ploughs were worn by abrasive silica and buckled by the hard layer beneath. Soil disturbances increased the rate of moisture loss; and as drought followed the rains the groundnuts were sealed into a brick-like mass.

Obviously, some savannas can be developed by careful planning; Kongwa now has experimental ranching. It may be that pastoral farming will be the most effective land-use over large areas. But this would call for control of numbers and quality of stock. Increased grazing intensity can have disastrous effects. In East Africa, overgrazed pastures tend to be invaded by a shrub, the Sodom Apple, which develops into dense thickets, sufficient to deter cattle, and is difficult to clear by burning. Again, small *Acacia* species, found naturally in grassland communities, tend to become denser in grazed areas, (page 29): in Kenya millions of hectares of grazing land have become seriously infested by thorn-bush. Even in moister savannas grazing has caused perennial grasses to be replaced by annuals and xerophytic succulents. As a result there is little dry season pasture, faster erosion, and, again, a spread of thorn-bush. Severe trampling can also lead to weed and thicket infestation.

Better management involves controlled grazing, for savanna grasses are most nutritive early in the rainy season, and there is a rapid decline in the percentage of crude protein content after that. With maturity, the grasses are more fibrous and less digestible. Hence continuous, moderate, controlled grazing or mowing is desirable. Nitrogen application improves most savanna pasture grasses. Where European breeds of cattle have been introduced, even greater investment is needed, for they are generally less tolerant of tropical conditions, and need more water, improved pastures, and disease precautions. But even with tribal herds, schemes can be devised to allow rest periods for pasture, if numbers are controlled: cattle dips and tsetse control can be set up, and the bush systematically cleared—with the additional bonus of providing charcoal.

In settled areas, farming is often best improved by introducing intermediate technology, giving technical advice, subsidising water schemes, fertilisers and pesticides, and providing marketing facilities.

Wildlife

The vast savanna areas are sparsely populated, but a large proportion of them shows the effects of man's interference. Man's activities impinge on the wildlife of the savannas, and modify and constrict its habitat, whether directed to exploit or conserve the natural environment. The complex symbiotic relationships between savanna lifeforms can scarcely be touched on here. In East Africa there is a broad ecological separation among the principal game animals, according to whether they graze or browse, what their water requirements are, and whether they eat dry or moist food. The separation of types of predator also partly responds to this distribution. In short grass savanna with a high proportion of *Acacia*, animals co-exist by selective grazing or browsing. Giraffe take *Acacia* leaves up to about five metres; rhino consume lower shoots of the whistling thorn; zebra take a high proportion of the taller grass stems; topi eat lower, upright grass blades, and wildebeeste the lower, near-horizontal blades. As a whole their grazing prevents the development of tree shoots, yet their consumption of fallen *Acacia* fruit helps to spread the plant.

During the dry season there are mass migratory movements away from the drier grasslands. In the case of zebra and wildebeeste this involves hundreds of thousands of animals whose hooves affect the soil surface. Other habits emphasise the complexity of savanna environments and their delicate balance. For example, a sandy patch may become a dust wallow for wildebeeste who so compact it that during the rains the depression retains water. The immediate vicinity of wallow and water hole, enriched by droppings, becomes an isolated micro-habitat, with flora and fauna differing from those of the surrounding savanna.

Fig. 17 A few trees and stark *Euphorbia* find nutrients in the cracks of a broken, jointed inselberg which is rounded by weathering. It stands above a savanna covered pediplain in southern Kenya, with whistling thorns among the tall grass. Typically, there is closer tree cover about the exposed mass itself.

IV The Effects of Morphogenic Processes

We have seen that savanna covers extensive surfaces of little relief, yet these include a variety of landforms. The alternating wet-dry tropics form a transition zone between the moist tropics and semi-arid conditions. There are, therefore, likely to be landforms akin to those found in these other zones. There are those which are characteristic of their present environment, and many which are modifications of landforms evolved under earlier climatic conditions.

Over hundreds of millions of years there have been cycles of pediplanation; so savannas occur on wide plainlands which are erosion surfaces at different heights. Each pediplanation cycle has involved the retreat of cliff-like features, whose weathered slopes retreat parallel to their face. The weathered material is removed by unconcentrated floods or wash from the foot of the slope. The break of the slope between the mountain face and the gently sloping pediment beneath is sharp,

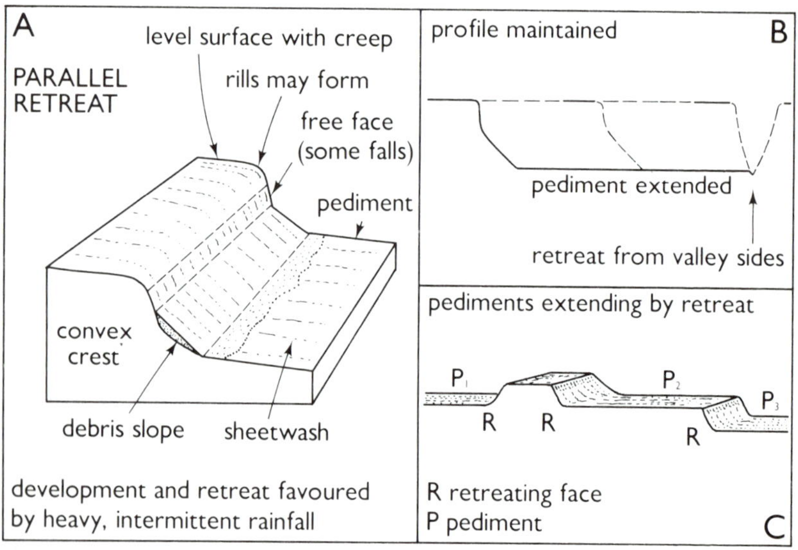

Fig. 18 A shows the processes acting to create and maintain the typical profile associated with the retreating edge of an escarpment or the faces of an exposed residual block. B shows the profile being maintained as retreat takes place, leaving an extending pediment. In C an earlier surface is preserved as a block standing between extending pediments P_1 and P_2. P_3 is being formed at the expense of P_2, perhaps initiated by a period of rejuvenation.

especially where weathering produces mainly small particles which are easily removed, such as sand from disintegrating granite. With such wash there is little erosion of the expanding pediment, but the smaller debris is spread outward over the adjacent plain.

On plateau lands the steep valley sides of the incised rivers have retreated in this way. Where the sides of different river valleys retreat towards each other, the plateau-like surface between them may ultimately be reduced to isolated inselbergs on the extending pediplain. These may eventually disintegrate. The processes acting to extend one surface at a lower level than another may eventually reduce the level of the latter.

Such plains, formed at different times and at different heights, are likely to bear very different plant associations. They may be part of a broad zone of savanna vegetation, but this is affected by past climatic influences, lithological differences, and the presence of scarp slopes beneath upper, level surfaces, or drainage systems whose broad valleys, or steep gorges, dissect the tablelands.

We must look again at the effects of high temperature and seasonal rainfall in promoting chemical weathering in areas of low relief, and at resulting landforms and soil conditions. Where sufficient moisture has allowed chemical weathering of the bedrock to proceed over a long period, deep regolith can form in areas of gentle relief, as in much of Uganda where the weathering of bedrock continues beneath a rotted layer 30–50 metres deep. If the hidden bedrock is strongly jointed, continuing chemical activity at the base of the regolith may divide the rock into blocks, which become rounded by such sub-surface weathering. Should a period of uplift, or climatic change, promote stream erosion and material transportation, much of the regolith may be removed; the exposed surface, with its large, separated, rounded rock masses, is now subjected to sub-aerial weathering. Such an exposed bedrock surface, with its irregularities, has been called an 'etchplain', and may in turn become deeply covered with weathered material—depending on climatic conditions. Renewed uplift would initiate a further cycle.

The length of time involved in such cycles is obviously great. So although present climatic conditions may seem not to favour such deep basal weathering, past conditions may well have produced the surfaces now exposed. It is likely that the processes described act successively, so that inselbergs on an etchplain may be reduced by parallel retreat, under conditions which do not at present favour deep chemical activity.

It is appropriate to look at the effects of duricrust formation on landscape features. Duricrusts often cover a large area, though not continuously. Differential erosion results in plateau-like features which, protected by their hard capping, stand above less-protected, eroded

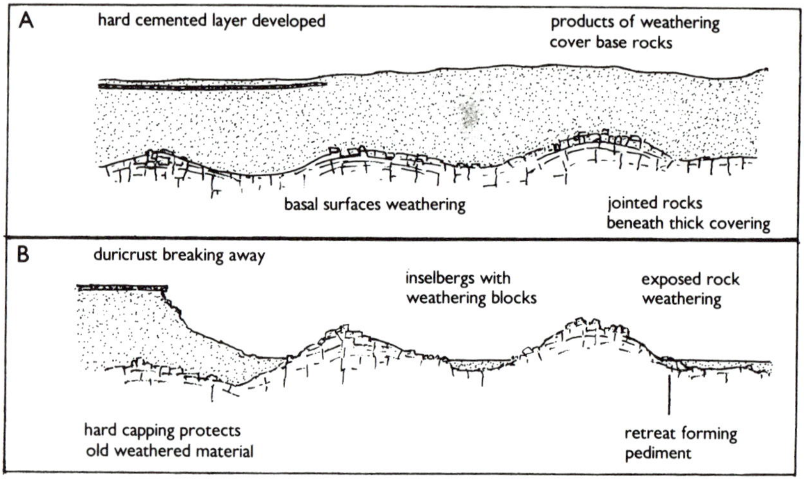

Fig. 19 In A the jointed rock lying beneath a thick cover of regolith is already weathering. In places, a hard indurated layer has developed near the surface. In B most of the old weathered material has been removed during a period of more effective erosion. Parts of the underlying jointed rock form inselbergs, exposed to sub-aerial weathering and retreat. The present surface includes accumulations of newly-weathered material and retreating mesa-like blocks protected by the old duricrust.

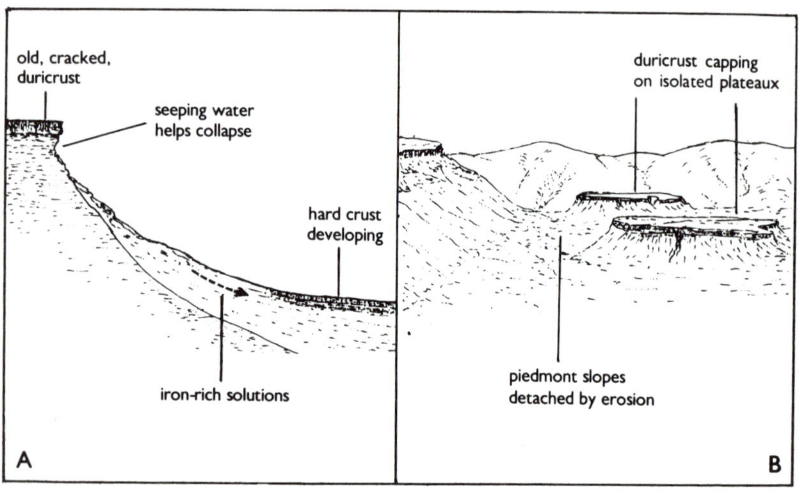

Fig. 20 In A water, which has permeated the old, cracked protective duricrust, seeps out at the face and helps the disintegration. A downward flow of iron-rich solutions allows a new hardened layer to form on less steep parts of the debris slope or on adjacent lowland. B shows that these, too, may in time form low, isolated, gently tilted blocks, below the level of the older features.

surfaces. However, duricrust formations sometimes create a landscape where separate mesa-like features stand *below* the general level of the surrounding hills or tablelands. Duricrusts often form in colluvial material or alluvial fans at the foot of uplands supplying iron-rich solutions. Hard layers tend to form in the lower, more gentle slopes, where there is a fluctuating water-table. As, in time, erosion separates these mounds of material from the highlands, they may stand out as slightly tilted, hard-capped blocks (Fig. 20). The iron-rich solutions are sometimes spread by run-off over wider areas of lowland, where infiltration, and subsequent evaporation creates duricrusts. Tectonic movements may raise these surfaces, so that rejuvenated erosion processes produce a landscape with outstanding, crust-protected blocks, subject to slow, parallel retreat. The adjacent uplands may, or may not, have ferricrete cappings.

A study of the selected regions which follow will clearly show how important geomorphological influences are in allowing particular forms of vegetation to become established; this may be seen in Fig. 21. Fig. 24 also emphasises the part they may play in creating a pattern of agricultural land-use and settlement.

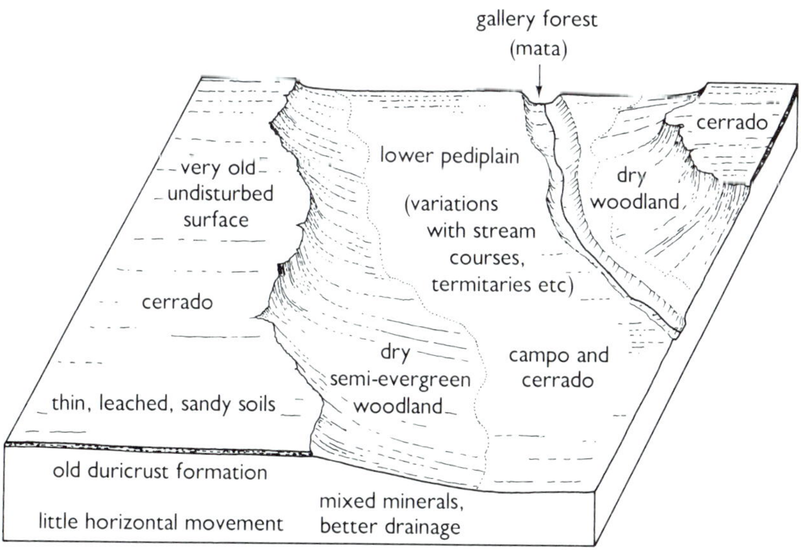

Fig. 21 A generalised picture of the sequence of soils and vegetation which may be found in eastern Brazil,[4] where old tablelands are retreating with pediplain formation, and where river courses cross the lower surfaces. In fact, other causes introduce further variations, and the vegetation associated with old termitaries or seasonal flood-hollows make for a patchy landscape; though the catenas illustrated occur over a wide area.

Features of Savanna Lands in Selected Areas

It is difficult to generalise about landforms produced over such a large part of the earth's surface. But it is possible to study a particular area and observe how the variables we have considered so far act to produce a recognisable pattern of relief features, soils, and vegetation. We can investigate relationships between internal variables of the soil and vegetation systems at selected locations, and look in turn at the external inputs and outputs of the Climatic, Lithological, Biotic/Human, and Morphogenic variables described above (I–IV in Fig. 2).

Two examples serve to show how varied savanna vegetation and associated forms of land-use may be. The first, from South America, shows that similar sequences of similar vegetation forms recur over a broad area. The second, from Africa, looks at significant patterns within a relatively small area. Each shows the development of catenas from upland surfaces to lower levels, with successions of soils in similar locations, and corresponding changes in vegetation, and the importance of past climatic and geomorphic conditions. The African example shows that savanna can occur in regions without seasonal drought.

Geomorphology and Catenas: Brazilian Savannas

Fig. 21 shows a generalised relationship between vegetation and geomorphology in eastern Brazil. The ancient, higher pediplain surfaces have soils which are old and exhausted, and where iron duricrusts are covered by shallow sandy soils, from a few centimetres to a metre or so in depth. The soils, already leached of their more soluble minerals are not readily removed from the level surfaces, and so replacement by weathering of the parent rock is very slow. Savanna grasses and low, twisted evergreen trees, with leathery leaves, thick bark and deep roots make up an edaphic climax vegetation, known as *campo cerrado* (see page 45). Plant species belonging to an ancient flora suggest a type of vegetation which was formerly more widespread.

At the retreating edges of the tablelands, and in valleys where soil removal allows the renewal of weathered material, there is a higher level of fertility and better drainage. Here forest may establish itself. It is usually a dry, semi-evergreen forest, with a close cover of slender trees and a canopy at some 15–18 metres. With a greater litter and higher organic content, the soils become more blocky and clayey.

Fig. 22 Campo cerrado covering a level plateau surface in eastern Brazil.[4] It is a mixture of tall grasses with many low, contorted trees with thick corky bark. The roseate clusters of large leaves are hard and leathery, and are retained during the dry season. Leaves may be lost at the end of winter, but not simultaneously.

Fig. 23 In the foreground campo cerrado covers a level surface of poor sandy soils.[4] Beyond, where the land begins to slope, there is an abrupt change. On the slopes, red sandy soils bear a more luxuriant form of savanna woodland, known as cerradão.

Stretching away below the slopes, with their colluvial material, is a lower pediplain, being extended at the expense of the higher tableland. Here, too, vegetation varies with the maturity of the soils, the extent of duricrust formation, and the ability of wash and rills to remove weathered products. A campo cerrado vegetation may be established, perhaps with close, taller woodland in depressions. Where a river valley, with a flowing stream and fine textured, poorly drained soils, crosses the plain, there is gallery rainforest (*mata*), with trees up to 40 metres, many with buttress roots.

Such a distribution of vegetation types in an area with broadly similar climatic conditions is seen mainly as a response to geomorphic evolution. There are, of course, responses to climatic variations over an area as large as the Brazilian tablelands. In the dry north-eastern parts the plateau surfaces bear *caatinga* vegetation, with thorny trees, low deciduous shrubs and spiny succulents. Here scarp slopes and more undulating country tend to support taller, dry deciduous forest, with large cacti and low *Euphorbia*. In some parts of the north-east, while caatinga covers the lower, extending pediplain surfaces, the isolated tablelands, receding by parallel retreat, bear campo cerrado, with its older flora.

Savanna without Seasonal Drought—Southern Uganda

The scenery of much of Buganda is made up of flat-topped hills, all about the same height, with gentle slopes leading down to broad valleys or lakes. Pre-Cambrian gneisses and schists form much of the country, and are usually deeply weathered.

The hills which lie some two kilometres north of Lake Victoria, near Entebbe, characteristically show remarkable similarities in their slope elements, in the soils and vegetation associated with these, and in the distribution of the local forms of land-use. Savanna covers much of the hills and hill slopes, despite the fact that there is not the more usual wet/dry seasonal climate of the 'savanna lands'. Figures for Entebbe show that there is no dry month, though a particularly wet period occurs between March and May, with another less pronounced one between October and December. The mean monthly temperatures are remarkably even, and so are the monthly absolute maxima and minima, never above 33°C, never below 12°C. The relative humidity in the early afternoon varies between 63 and 74 per cent.

Entebbe: mean figures (0°04 N) 1180 metres

	J	F	M	A	M	J	J	A	S	O	N	D	Annual
Temperature (°C)	22	22	22	22	21	21	20	21	21	21	22	21	—
Rainfall (mm)	65	90	158	253	240	120	75	72	72	91	130	115	1480

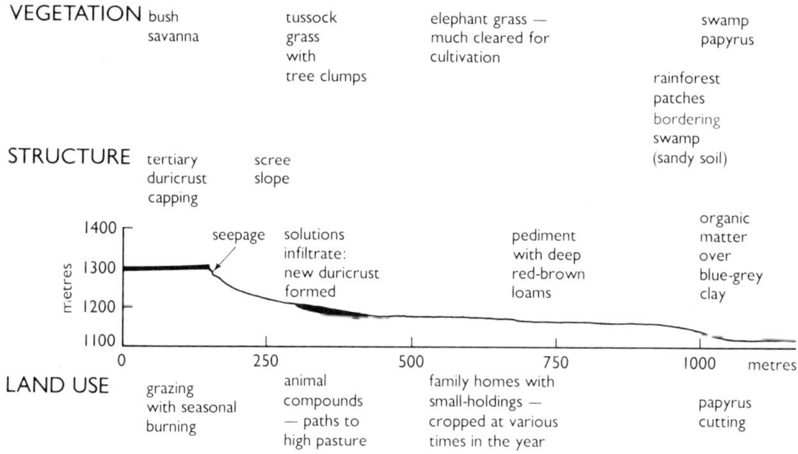

Fig. 24 A summary of the physical processes and soil-vegetation catenas associated with the retreat of elevated surfaces to the north of Lake Victoria. The general responses in land-use are shown.

Fig. 24 shows the typical slope elements.[5] The flat hill-top stands at 1300 metres and has a duricrust, iron-rich layer; this falls slightly at its edges, where soil movements have taken place and where sagging occurs, due to the emergence of water which has infiltrated fissures in the crust. Grasses cover the hill top surface.

Below the edge of the duricrust, its fragments, in a clayey matrix, form a scree slope of between 20–25°, falling some 30 metres. This is covered by tussock grass, though tree clumps occur about places of active seepage from beneath the duricrust. Below this is the pediment, with a typically constant gradient of some 7°, and with a slight concavity. Deep red-brown loams develop on these slopes, covered in the natural state by dense elephant grass. In places the lower parts of the pediment have hard duricrusts developed from the infiltration and evaporation of iron-rich solutions received from above.

The valleys below have alluvial soils and are mostly swampy. Patches of rainforest grow on light sandy loams at the fringe of swamps, with their tall papyrus.

Here, then, in a smaller area, is a catena sequence, from the high duricrust layer, probably formed in Tertiary times under drier conditions, to the young swamp soils, which when drained are black over a bluish-grey clay. The vegetation forms associated with this are thus responding to past and present climatic conditions, and to slopes, drainage, and soils, the characteristics of which are responses to environmental changes over a period of time. Today, the evenly distributed rainfall helps to preserve a vegetation cover which retains soil on slopes, helps to preserve soil structure, reduces sheet wash, and minimises rill formation.

Finally we see human activities modifying the natural vegetation. The hill tops are grazed by cattle and goats, and at times the grasses and low shrubs are burnt, which helps to maintain the grassland and improve pasture quality. At the lowest part of the catena, the swamp soils, with their high organic content, support only papyrus, which is little used, except for handicrafts. In between, the deep soils of the pediment are cultivated for a variety of crops, planted at intervals throughout the year—maize, sweet potatoes and beans in the wettest period, and later cotton, millet and cassava. Bananas are established, and picked throughout the year, and coffee grown as a cash crop. Each hill is thus ringed by a belt of small-holdings, often with animal compounds in the zone immediately above, and a maze of paths running to the high pastures. 'Natural vegetation' has, in fact, little meaning here—but the maintenance of the *pattern* of land-use depends on the stability of the soil systems in the various parts of the catena.

After seeing two cases where there are catena developments and regular, recognisable patterns of vegetation, we turn to two continental areas which illustrate the difficulties of delimiting forms of savanna vegetation and accounting for their present distribution.

Difficulties in Classification—Australian Savannas

Fig. 25 shows areas of savanna woodland, tree savanna, and dry savanna grassland, with peripheral forests, a large part of the dry interior covered by forms of mallee (*Eucalyptus*) or mulga (*Acacia*) scrub, and an interior desert by no means devoid of vegetation.

The present rainforests are relics of much more extensive forests during wetter periods in the Pleistocene. They are now restricted to near-coastal locations in the east. The others are tall eucalypt forests, with ferns in moist locations and sclerophyllous shrubs in drier ones. Towards the interior, to the west of the eastern ranges and in far south-west, the eucalypts form a canopy over grasses, while further inland the trees space out to form savanna woodland. The evergreen eucalypts persist far inland—hundreds of species with deep roots, oily stems and leaves, twisting leaf-stems, fire-resistant seed cases and other adaptations survive in the very dry country. The borders between forest, savanna woodland, and savanna grassland are blurred.

The dominant grasses vary. Tall, perennial Flinders and Mitchell grasses, modified by grazing, extend from the black earth zone of east central Queensland into the sub-tropics in New South Wales and Victoria. Tussocky grasses form a more arid savanna from western Queensland to the northern parts of Western Australia. In Northern Territory this shades northwards into a tall-grass, close tree country, with many termitaries. In the interior, however, the vegetation distribution is complex. In places mallee and mulga forms are associated almost entirely with drought-resistant shrubs; yet, elsewhere, they occur with tussock grassland. Even in the centre, the grasslands west of Alice Springs support grazing. The rainfall is unreliable, however, and this greatly affects plant behaviour. During the 1970s, exceptional rains over large parts of central Australia produced unusually luxuriant plant foliage.

Over much of the continent relief variations are slight. There are obvious responses to rainfall amounts and seasonal distribution; but lithological differences, soil variations, plant inter-actions, and increasing human interference make generalisations unreliable, and stress the need for close, scientific study of any particular habitat. (p. 45).

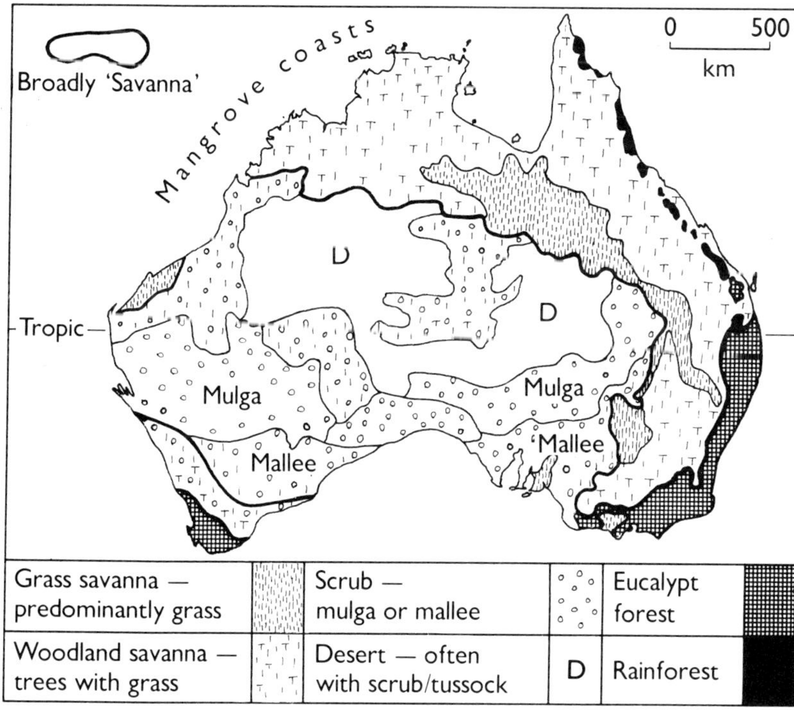

Fig. 25 The map stresses the difficulty of establishing what constitutes 'savanna'. In the interior, wide areas of semi-desert scrub with sparse tussock grass include stretches of well-grassed country with low trees; the peripheral forests also include patches of grassland; and the tree density of the northern savanna-woodland varies enormously. Over most of the interior a decade or more of drought may be followed by a similar period with exceptional rains, converting semi-desert into apparently rich tropical grassland.

Fig. 26 During mid-summer this woodland savanna, just south of Darwin, is a bright green landscape of tall grasses, thin eucalypts of moderate height, and spiky pandanus. Most of the mean annual rainfall of 1500 mm falls at this time.

Fig. 27 Fifteen hundred kilometres south of Darwin, in the heart of Australia, is a cattle raising area with plains of mulga (*Acacia* spp.), mixed shrubs and spinifex (*Triodia* spp.). The spinifex may be burnt to promote new growth. This tropical landscape amid the Macdonnell Ranges has less than 300 mm of rain a year, as an average, but received far in excess of that during the mid-1970s.

Fig. 28 Deccan scenery, in the lee of India's Western Ghats, during the dry, cooler season, with its dusty earth roads and straw-coloured landscape. The climatic regime would seem to favour some kind of grassland—some 800 mm of rain falls between May and September; but, obviously, the present plant associations on uncultivated land are due to anthropogenic as well as climatic causes.

Dominant Anthropogenic Factors—Savannas of the Indian Deccan

Over thousands of years, men clearing land for scattered patches of cultivation and the practice of unregulated grazing have converted vast areas of the Deccan to a short-grass savanna with scattered trees. East of the Western Ghats the annual rainfall over most of the plateau averages between 500 and 1000 mm; but there is little rain for eight months in the year, and, with noon temperatures about 25°C in the cool season and over 40°C in the hot, evaporation rates are high. In the lee of the Ghats, and in the dry central parts of the plateau, it is likely that climatic climax thorn-bush savanna formed the natural vegetation. But the low thorny *Acacia* and tussocky grasses which cover uncultivated parts of the volcanic soils of the Deccan has probably degraded from dry deciduous forest.

In such circumstances, descriptions of natural vegetation are academic, for the landscapes are essentially human. Fig. 28 shows that in

Fig. 29 Close woodland covers the low outcrops and the steep debris slopes below the free-face of these weathered ridges in western Thailand. There is an annual rainfall of some 1300 mm and a short dry period in mid-winter. Permanent fields lie along the summer flood area of the seasonal watercourses; but elsewhere shifting cultivation and grazing have created an open landscape of grasses and isolated trees.

the dry season small fields, rough pasture, earth roads, and even the small villages merge into a drab, dusty landscape, where the occasional bulkier banyan tree or darker mango stands out above the thorny *Acacia*. Even if man's activities are peripheral to, or scattered within, large areas of uncultivated countryside, the dispersal of cultivated plants, and changes in the water-table of a partly occupied basin, add to the more obvious modifications caused by foraging for wood, itinerant grazing, or transverse pathways. Climatic and geomorphic controls are still significant, but anthropogenic factors affect the form of vegetation, whether savanna or otherwise.

Other parts of south-east Asia have also been converted from semi-deciduous forest to forms of savanna. The seasonal droughts and soil conditions of parts of central Burma and Indo-China have much influence on the presence of savanna, but the effects of shifting cultivation, lumbering, and clearance for semi-permanent cultivation are also responsible for the present widespread, if discontinuous, occurrence of savanna within these countries (Figs 28 and 29).

The Value of Simplification and the Need for Analysis of Field Data

These case studies have indicated some reasons for regularities of soil-vegetation distribution—where there are catenas, for example. They also suggest that, in view of the variations which can exist within savanna formations, precise field studies are needed in order to appreciate the relationships between topography, soil conditions, and particular forms of savanna. Field workers must first assess which variables are likely to provide significant data for analysis. We have seen the value of simple models which select small working parts of a complex system in order to concentrate in turn on significant variables.

This is illustrated by Fig. 30, which considers again soil nutrient status, so important to plant development. A shows simply that the weathering of the rocks releases nutrients, and considers certain broad

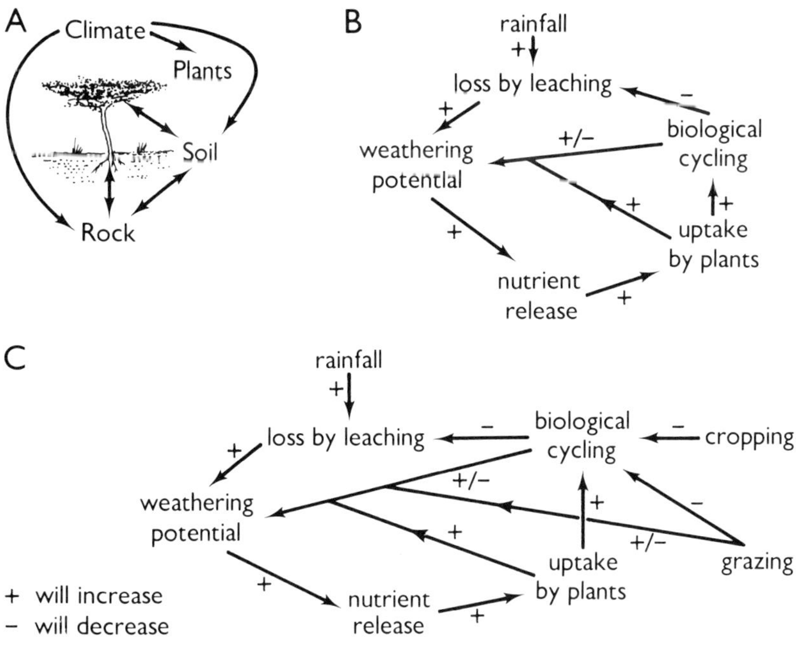

Fig. 30 Simple diagrams which isolate and examine processes taking place in more complex systems.

inter-actions. B takes into consideration nutrient loss from the system by drainage. This can cause additional nutrient release, and progressive losses cause progressive release, which may eventually lower the nutrient status of the system. This simple diagram shows other relationships, such as the positive and negative influences of biological cycling on weathering. C expresses, in addition, the effects of cropping and grazing, and points to the fact that there is a return as well as removal of nutrients, in part directly from grazing animals, but possibly by a chain of events affecting nutrient release from rock.

Such models express likely relationships in general terms, but can reflect only a small part of the actual conditions and processes. In the field it may be found that the nutrient release by particular rocks is low, as with many sandstones and siliceous shales, or high, as in the case of basalt. The nature of the soils may reflect a certain stage of maturity—an old profile with near-surface mineral deficiency, or poorly structured recent accumulation with potential fertility. A systems model may focus attention on a variable and its likely influences, but the actual role it plays may only be revealed by detailed study in the field (which, in time, may lead to modification of the model).

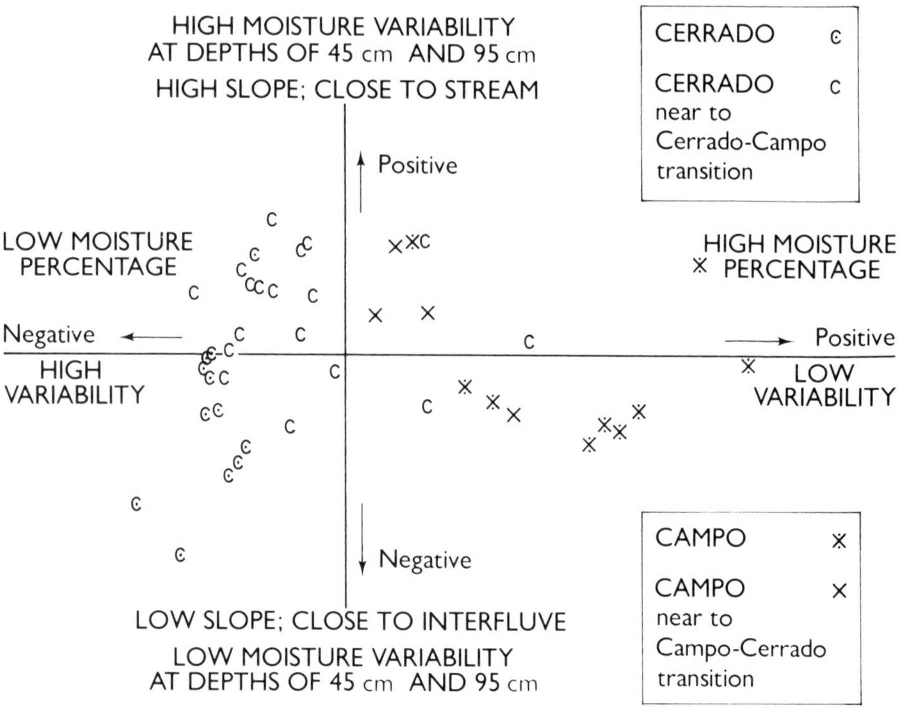

Fig. 31 Relations between soil moisture, topography, vegetation types (campo and cerrado) at 43 monthly sampled sites in Mato Grosso, Brazil.[6]

Field data assembled over a period of time may be arranged and analysed[6] so as to give an insight into causal factors. But even this may be only one stage in a complete study. It may provide a clearer picture for renewed field investigation or laboratory simulation.

In the context of savanna forms, Fig. 31 shows the result of a graphical technique involving component analysis, which apparently points to significantly different relationships between chosen environmental factors and forms of vegetation in eastern Brazil. Here *campo* refers to open grassland and *cerrado* to 'bush' savanna with a tangle of shrubs. The variables at selected sites in Mato Grosso were sampled monthly, and are seen on the graph to be distributed in two axes, so that the scatter of points (shown here by symbols) represents a correlation between the variates. This suggests reasons for the distribution of campo and cerrado, and also indicates conditions which favour a mingling of the forms of vegetation in places marginal to main areas of campo and cerrado. For instance, cerrado is seen to occur on sites with low moisture values, high moisture variability, well above stream level, and close to a watershed, with low slope values. A general picture of the distribution of these associations was obtained, but other forms of analysis were used to consider the influence of specific local geomorphological features.

There are, thus, a number of very different, but complementary, processes that help us understand these complex systems, which, despite their variety, come under the heading 'Tropical Savannas'. They form a sequence: Observations and Field Measurements → Simplification with Systems Models → Exact Field Study and Analysis → Modification of Models.

References

[1]M. THOMAS (1971) Savanna Lands between Desert and Forest *Geog. Mag.* **44** p. 185
[2]R. A. PULLAN (1975) Burning Impact on African Savannas *Geog. Mag.* **47** p. 432
[3]M. M. COLE (1963) Vegetation and Geomorphology in Northern Rhodesia *Geog. Journal* **129** p. 290
[4]M. M. COLE (1960) Distribution and Origin of Savanna Vegetation in Brazil *Geog. Journal* **126** p. 168
[5]J. W. PALLISER (1956) Slope Development in Buganda *Geog. Journal* **122** p. 80
[6]S. G. DAULTREY (1970) An Analysis of the Relation between Soil Moisture, Topography, and Vegetation Types in a Savanna Area *Geog. Journal* **136** p. 399

Other Sources

A. S. COLLINSON (1980) Introduction to World Vegetation (Allen and Unwin)
S. R. EYRE (1975) Vegetation and Soils (Arnold)
B. HOPKINS (1974) Forest and Savanna (Heinemann)
D. C. MONEY (1978) Climate, Soils and Vegetation (UTP)
N. POLUNIN (1960) Introduction to Plant Geography (Longman)
J. TIVY (1979) Biogeography (Oliver and Boyd)
J. TRICART (1972) Landforms of the Humid Tropics, Forest, and Savannas (Longman)
S. T. TRUDGILL (1977) Soil and Vegetation Systems (Oxford)
H. WALTER (1979) Vegetation of the Earth (Springer-Verlag)

Points for Discussion

1 The validity of using 'savanna' as a blanket term for a tropical vegetation formation.

2 The concept that the removal of nutrients from a soil nutrient system will act to encourage the release of further cations by the weathering of primary minerals.

3 The relationship between mean annual rainfall and types of savanna vegetation.

4 Dominant influences on the proportion of herbaceous plants, shrubs and trees in various forms of savanna.

5 Reasons for similar catena formations over wide areas within the tropics.

6 Factors governing infiltration and run-off, and their effects on selected savanna areas.

7 The significance of cuirassing processes (duricrust formation) to tropical landforms and associated types of vegetation.

8 Similarities in the landforms of present-day savannas in Africa and South America.

9 The importance of recognising the influences of past climatic conditions on present soil structure and land formations.

10 The significance of the fact that the biomass of soil animals and vertebrates is often very large in savanna lands. (East African figures show 250 kg per hectare for soil animals in thorn-bush and 100–300 kg per hectare for vertebrate herbivores.)

11 The dangers of absolute protection of life-forms in large conservation areas.

12 The effects of the increasing human population on the world's tropical grasslands.

13 The advantages and disadvantages of periodic firing of types of savanna vegetation.

14 The likelihood of developing savanna lands for purposes other than a pastoral economy.

15 The need for time to make *progressive* studies of significant variables affecting a particular stretch of savanna.

Glossary

anaerobic without free oxygen
anthropogenic created through human action
biotic pertaining to life
catena a sequence of soil types from top to bottom of a slope, developed in similar positions under similar circumstances
climax community the final, relatively permanent, form of vegetation developed under local climatic and soil conditions
colloid molecules of a solute grouped together in a mobile state (sol) or stable state (gel)
colluvium mixed mineral particles moved and deposited by creep or wash through the influence of gravity
cuirasse a surface, or near-surface crust, hardened by infiltrating solutions which leave cementing minerals
duricrust (see cuirasse)
ecosystem a complex integrated system in which living communities and their non-living environment interact
evapo-transpiration the combined loss of water from surfaces and by transpiration from plants
ferricrete a hard surface, or sub-surface layer, whose mineral particles are cemented by iron compounds
ferruginous rich in iron compounds
flocculation linking particles into aggregates
geomorphic related to the shape of landforms
hardpan a cemented or compacted layer at, or below, the surface
humus a substance produced by the slow decomposition and oxidation of organic matter on, or near, the surface
illuviation redeposition of colloidal material after removal from another soil horizon
inselberg a steep-sided, isolated hill—often a tropical residual
inter-pluvial a drier spell between particularly rainy periods
ion an atom, or group of atoms, positively charged through losing electrons (cation) or negatively charged through gaining electrons (anion)
leaching removal of soil materials in solution by percolating water
lithological related to the structure and composition of rocks
mesophytic vegetation adapted to moderately moist conditions
morphogenic related to the evolution of specific landforms
nitrifying conversion of nitrogen or nitrogen compounds to substances which can be used in biological processes
pediment gently sloping, debris strewn, eroded rock platform adjoining a scarp face or mountain slope
pediplain an almost flat erosion surface comprising extended pediments formed by scarp retreat
photosynthesis the conversion of carbon dioxide and water into organic compounds by solar energy and plant chlorophyll
protoplasm the fluid making up the cells of living organisms; it contains proteins
pyrophyte a plant adapted to survive the regular occurrence of fire
regolith a mantle of debris and material weathered from and covering the bed-rock
sesquioxide compounds in which two metallic atoms are combined with three oxygen atoms—Fe_2O_3 and Al_2O_3
sclerophyllous having organs with thickened cell walls to protect against the loss of water
siliceous formed of silica
sub-aerial under atmospheric influences
succulent a plant which stores water in its tissues
symbiotic associated inter-dependent life forms—living together for their own advantage
tectonic related to movements of the earth's crust
tussock tufted grasses growing in compact clumps
ungulate a hoofed mammal
xeromorphic structure which enables a plant to survive despite a limited water supply
xerophytic vegetation adapated to dry environmental conditions